ZEALOUS
for Good Works

Heath Rogers

ONESTONE
BIBLICAL RESOURCES

2024 One Stone Press.
All rights reserved. No part of this book may be reproduced in any form without written permission of the publisher.

Published by:
One Stone Press
979 Lovers Lane
Bowling Green, KY 42103

Printed in the United States of America

ISBN (13 Digit): 978-1-941422-83-0

1 (800) 428-0121
www.onestone.com

Contents

Part One - Zealous

Lesson 1	Christ Makes Us Zealous for Good Works	7
Lesson 2	The Proper Source for Zeal	11
Lesson 3	Zealous for the Right Things	15
Lesson 4	Protecting Our Zeal	19
Lesson 5	The Zeal of Jesus	23
Lesson 6	The Zeal of Paul – part one	27
Lesson 7	The Zeal of Paul – part two	31

Part Two – Good Works

Lesson 8	Spreading the Gospel	37
Lesson 9	Encouraging Others	43
Lesson 10	Helping Those in Need	49
Lesson 11	Singing	55
Lesson 12	Praying	59
Lesson 13	Helping the Sick and the Grieving	63

Dedication

This book is dedicated to our good friends Paul and Anna Linden. Their constant love, encouragement, and support through the years is one of the many blessings my wife Christy and I enjoy.

Introduction

"Looking for the blessed hope and glorious appearing of our great God and Savior Jesus Christ, who gave Himself for us, that He might redeem us from every lawless deed and purify for Himself His own special people, zealous for good works" (Titus 2:13-14).

Paul left the young evangelist Titus on the island of Crete (Titus 1:5). This island's inhabitants were notorious for being "liars, evil beasts, and lazy gluttons" (v. 12). The Christians on Crete had to break away from this sinful way of life. Throughout the remainder of the epistle, Paul emphasized the need for them to be zealous for good works.

Many Christians struggle with maintaining zeal for the good works. This workbook addresses this need among God's people today. The first half of the book is a study of different aspects of zeal, with special attention given to the examples of our Lord and the apostle Paul. The second half of the book is a practical study of some of the good works we need to be performing with zeal.

I am extremely grateful for Carolyn Bixby taking the time to proofread this material. Her zeal in accomplishing this task was shown in the fact that she proofread the last lesson I wrote while she was recovering from a fractured hip! Many of her suggestions are a part of this workbook.

Unless otherwise noted, all Bible quotations are from the New King James Version.

Christ Makes Us Zealous for Good Works

Lesson 1

"Who gave Himself for us, that He might redeem us from every lawless deed and purify for Himself His own special people, zealous for good works" (Titus 2:14).

Zeal is defined as "a strong feeling of interest and enthusiasm that makes someone very eager or determined to do something"(www.merriam-webster.com/dictionary/zeal).

In the New Testament, the words zeal and zealous come from a root Greek word that means to be hot or heated; to boil as a liquid, or to glow as a solid. Think of the energy seen in a pot of boiling water or felt from a roaring campfire. This is the image we should have in mind when we think of being zealous. Zeal is a burning passion that results in action.

Zeal, like fire, lies in the realm of moral neutrality. Fire, in and of itself, is neither good nor bad. It can be used to accomplish good or to destroy. Zeal is the same. It can be expressed as envy or jealousy, which results in sin. It can also be the passion that motivates us to perform the "good works" God created us to accomplish (Titus 2:14; Eph. 2:10).

For faithful Christians, zeal is a burning passion to serve and please God.

It appears that some Christians are naturally zealous. Zeal is a part of their character. This doesn't mean the rest of us can't be zealous. The title of this study comes from the last sentence in Titus 2:14. It is our Savior, Jesus Christ, who makes us zealous for good works. Let's take a close look at this verse and see exactly how Jesus provides us with the adequate spark to ignite our zeal and keep it burning.

1. Jesus Gave Himself for Us

Our Lord's suffering and death on the cross were *voluntary*. No one made Jesus go to the cross. He exercised the choice given to Him by the Father.

> "Therefore My Father loves Me, because I lay down My life that I may take it again. No one takes it from Me, but I lay it down of Myself. I have power to lay it down, and I have power to take it again. This command I have received from My Father" (John 10:17-18).

He chose to die for us out of love and pity for our souls (John 15:13).

His death was also a *sacrificial* act. He died in our place. He tasted death (the penalty for sin) on our behalf (Heb. 2:9; Gal. 1:4). As has been beautifully said—"He paid a debt He didn't owe because we owed a debt we couldn't pay."

We honor those who make voluntary sacrifices for others, especially those who personally make such sacrifices for us. Jesus deserves this kind of honor. Gratitude for what Jesus did for us demands that we give ourselves entirely to Him, doing what He wants us to do – being zealous for good works.

2. Jesus Redeems Us

The word *redeem* in the Greek New Testament is terminology from the world of slavery. It means to set one free by payment of a ransom, to liberate, or to rescue.

Jesus came to accomplish this important work. "For even the Son of Man did not come to be served, but to serve, and to give His life a ransom for many" (Mark 10:45; c.f. 1 Tim. 2:6). The ransom price was His own blood (1 Pet. 1:18-19).

From what are we redeemed? Christians are redeemed "from every lawless deed" (NKJV), "from all iniquity" (KJV), "from all lawlessness" (ESV). This is another way the Bible speaks of our sin. "Whoever commits sin also commits lawlessness, and sin is lawlessness" (1 John 3:4). Lawlessness is acting without regard for God's law and authority. Therefore, sin is lawlessness.

Sin has a binding and enslaving power. Jesus sets us free from sin's bondage (John 8:34-36).

Paul told Titus that Jesus redeems us from "*every* lawless deed," "*all* iniquity," "*all* lawlessness." His sacrifice is sufficient and complete. He is the only Savior and Redeemer we will ever need. There is no one else to whom we can turn. No one else can help us escape the bondage of and penalty for our sins. We owe Jesus everything for our spiritual freedom from sin. Is it too much for Him to ask that we be zealous for His good works?

3. Jesus Purifies Us

There is another blessing that comes from our Lord's suffering and death. His shed blood not only delivers us from sin's bondage, but it also *cleans-*

es us from its stain. Sin contaminates. "'Come now, and let us reason together,' says the Lord, 'Though your sins are like scarlet, they shall be as white as snow; though they are red like crimson, they shall be as wool'" (Isa. 1:18).

Sin's stain separates mankind from a holy God. The Bible could have ended with Genesis chapter three. God could have let us go in our sin, and He would have been justified in doing so, but His great love for us would not allow Him to just let us go. He sent His Son as the atonement for our sins (Rom. 5:6-11). Jesus volunteered to be our sacrifice. How can we think about this great blessing and not be zealous to serve the Lord?

4. Jesus Purifies Us to Be His Own Special People

By cleansing us from our sins, Jesus makes us different from the rest of mankind. We become "His own special people" (NKJV), "a peculiar people" (KJV), "a people for his own possession" (NASV, ESV).

Everything belongs to Christ (Col. 1:16), but Christians are His in a special sense. We have been sanctified, or set apart, from the rest of the people in the world (1 Cor. 1:2; Heb. 10:10). We are to come out and be separate from the sinful world around us (2 Cor. 6:17-18). We have been purchased with Christ's blood (1 Cor. 6:19-20). He bought us for a purpose: to glorify God by being zealous for good works.

Conclusion

Christians are saved people, but we are saved for a purpose. We are to express our gratitude for what Jesus did for us by zealously doing those things He would have us do.

We are to be zealous for good works—not occasionally zealous, not when it is convenient for us. Christians are to be characterized by zeal. We are to be committed to serving the Lord with energy and enthusiasm.

Zeal is a fire every Christian should keep burning in his heart. What is the spark that ignites and maintains this flame? The more time we spend meditating on what Jesus has already done for us, the easier it will be to maintain our zeal to do His good works.

Questions

1. What is zeal? _____
   _____

2. Explain how zeal is like a fire. _____
   _____

3. In what sense was our Lord's crucifixion a voluntary act (John 10:17-18; 15:13)? _____
   _____

4. Describe how our Lord's death was a sacrificial act (Heb. 2:9; Gal. 1:4).
   _____
   _____

5. Define the word redeem. _____
   _____

6. What price did Jesus pay to redeem us from our sins (1 Pet. 1:18-19)?
   _____

7. What motivated God to send His Son to die for our sins (Rom. 5:8)? ___
   _____

8. What sanctifies, or sets us apart, from the sinful world (Heb. 10:10)? ___
   _____

9. According to Titus 2:14, why does Jesus have the right to expect us to be zealous for good works? _____
   _____

The Proper Source for Zeal

Lesson 2

Zeal can be defined as great energy or enthusiasm in pursuit of a cause or objective. The word *zeal*, as used in the New Testament, is translated from the Greek word *zelos*, which means to be hot or to heat. This study likens zeal to a fire.

We learn an important lesson about the source of fire from Nadab and Abihu. "Then Nadab and Abihu, the sons of Aaron, each took his censer and put fire in it, put incense on it, and offered profane fire before the Lord, which He had not commanded them. So fire went out from the Lord and devoured them, and they died before the Lord" (Lev. 10:1-2). These men were authorized to offer incense to God on the altar, but He struck them dead because they got the fire from the wrong source.

One attitude in religion is that it really doesn't matter where we get our zeal, just as long as we are zealous. Who cares why a Christian is enthusiastic or passionate about serving Christ? Does it matter how the fire started or what sustains it? Shouldn't we just be thankful they want to serve the Lord?

If we want our zeal (fire) to accomplish good for the cause of Christ (to be "zealous for good works"- Titus 2:14), and if we want it to last and not burn out, it must come from the right source. The Bible reveals proper sources for a Christian's zeal.

Understanding God's Word

"Brethren, my heart's desire and prayer to God for Israel is that they may be saved. For I bear them witness that they have a zeal for God, but not according to knowledge" (Rom. 10:1-2).

Devout Jews had a zeal for God. They exhibited this zeal through their efforts to crucify Jesus and persecute His apostles. Regardless, they were lost because their zeal was not according to a knowledge of God's word.

Many people claim to be Christians. Some of them are very zealous about exercising their religious beliefs. However, they are also lost because their zeal is not based on knowledge (a proper understanding of God's word).

In Luke 24, we read that Jesus appeared to two disciples who were on the road to Emmaus (vv. 13-35). They did not recognize Jesus. He asked why they were sad. They did not understand that the Christ had to be crucified and risen from the dead. Jesus corrected their understanding of the Scriptures. "Then beginning with Moses and with all the prophets, He explained to them the things concerning Himself in all the Scriptures" (Luke 24:27, NASU).

The word *explained* is from the Greek word *diermeneuo* which means "to unfold the meaning of what is said" (Thayer 147). I like that definition. It paints a good picture for us. To properly understand God's word, we have to open it, unfold it, and dig into it. This requires effort.

Notice what these two men said about Jesus unfolding God's word to them. "And they said to one another, 'Did not our heart burn within us while He talked with us on the road, and while He opened the Scriptures to us?'" (Luke 24:32). Their understanding of the Scriptures kindled fire in their hearts. The same thing can happen to us, but only if we invest ourselves and our time by studying God's word to understand His will for our lives today.

True Repentance

Satan uses anything he can to quench our zeal. Nothing extinguishes the fire of a Christian's zeal like sin and guilt. Note what David said about the burden of his guilt. "When I kept silent, my bones grew old through my groaning all the day long. For day and night Your hand was heavy upon me; my vitality was turned into the drought of summer" (Psa. 32:3-4). David's strength and passion were gone.

True repentance brings forgiveness, joy, and zeal. The church in Corinth had many problems. Paul's first letter addressed these problems and how to solve them. News came back to Paul that some of the Corinthians had responded in repentance. Their repentance produced diligence, indignation, vehement desire, and zeal (2 Cor. 7:8-11).

We all sin. Our pride tempts us to hide our sins and pretend they didn't happen. If we do so, our guilt can extinguish our zeal. The proper way to handle the guilt of sin is to repent, confess our sins to God, and pray for forgiveness (Acts 8:22; 1 John 1:9). Doing so will bring God's forgiveness and help revive our zeal.

Zealous Brethren

Paul told the Corinthians that their Macedonian brethren were very much involved in the Lord's work (2 Cor. 8:1-5). He spoke of the abundance of their joy and the riches of their liberality despite their great trial of affliction and deep poverty. They were freely willing, beyond their ability, desiring with much urgency to participate in the collection for the needy saints. These Macedonian Christians were on fire!

Where did their zeal originate? "Now concerning the ministering to the saints, it is superfluous for me to write to you; for I know your willingness, about which I boast of you to the Macedonians, that Achaia was ready a year ago; and *your zeal has stirred up the majority*" (2 Cor. 9:1-2, emphasis mine - HR). Paul had told them that the Corinthians were already participating in this effort. Their zeal stirred up the Macedonians.

Fire is contagious. It can easily spread from one place to another. The same is true of godly zeal. God, in His wisdom, has put believers together in local churches so that their zeal can be kept burning by brethren sharing in the effort. Look to those who are actively involved in the work of the church. Spend time with them. Let their zeal light a fire in you.

Conclusion

It does matter where we get our zeal. If we are to be "zealous for good works" (Titus 2:14), the fire needs to motivate us to do God's work in God's way, and we need to keep the fire burning.

Christians can get excited by listening to false doctrine, focusing on the good while ignoring sin, and being around the wrong people. This short-lived excitement can lead us in the wrong direction. Zeal's fire is properly ignited by a true understanding of God's word, true repentance, and the influence of zealous brethren.

References

Thayer, Joseph H., "Thayer's Greek-English Lexicon of the New Testament," Peabody, Massachusetts, Hendrickson Publishers, 1996, print.

Questions

1. The Jews had zeal, but not according to knowledge of God's word (Rom. 10:1-2). What was the source of their zeal? Consider Paul's statement in Galatians 1:14 in your answer. _____

_____

2. How did Jesus help the two disciples on the road to Emmaus (Luke 24:27)? _____
_____

3. How did these disciples react to the Lord's teaching (v. 32)? _____
_____

4. What efforts are required to properly understand God's word (2 Tim. 2:15; Heb. 5:12-14; Psa. 1:2)? _____
_____
_____

5. How can guilt due to personal sin quench our zeal (Psa. 32:3-4)? _____
_____
_____

6. Can true repentance revive zeal (2 Cor. 7:8-11)? Why or why not? __
_____
_____
_____

7. What are Christians to do for one another (Heb. 10:24)? _____
_____

8. Why were the poor Christians in Macedonia willing to give so generously (2 Cor. 9:1-2)? _____
_____

9. What are some dangerous (improper) sources of zeal for a Christian? __
_____
_____

Zealous for the Right Things

Lesson 3

Zeal is great energy or enthusiasm exerted in the pursuit of a cause or objective. In our previous lesson, we saw that zeal must come from the proper source. This lesson shows that zeal must be directed toward the proper things.

Zeal lies in the realm of moral neutrality. It is energy, enthusiasm, or passion that motivates us to do great good or great harm. Using a car to illustrate, we see that zeal is the fuel that fires the engine and propels the vehicle. However, for the car to arrive at its intended destination, the steering must also function properly.

False teachers were troubling the churches in Galatia. They were "zealously" courting these Christians to follow their errors. In exposing these false teachers, Paul acknowledged their zeal but stated that it was pointed in the wrong direction. He told the Galatians, "...it is good to be zealous in a *good thing* always" (Gal. 4:17-18, emphasis mine - HR).

What are these good things? How can we identify them? In the second half of this book, we will discuss some specific things we are to perform with zeal. However, in this lesson, we examine three things we can do to ensure we are pointed in the right direction and remain zealous for good works.

1. Christians Should Know Right from Wrong

"Abhor what is evil. Cling to what is good" (Rom. 12:9). We need to know the difference between *evil* and *good*, because the way we react to and approach each one is different.

God's word is the standard that establishes good and evil. "The entirety of Your word is truth, and every one of Your righteous judgments endures forever" (Psa. 119:160). Christians gain understanding from learning and using God's word. As we learn and grow, we apply the Scriptures to our lives and thereby gain the ability to "discern both good and evil" (Heb. 5:12-14).

Zealously doing good works requires us to know right from wrong as determined by God's word. Paul told Timothy, "All Scripture is given by inspiration of God, and is profitable for doctrine, for reproof, for correction, for instruction in righteousness, that the man of God may be complete, thoroughly equipped for every good work" (2 Tim. 3:16-17). The Scriptures give instruction in righteousness, which equips us for every good work.

2. Christians Should Know What is Best

In Luke 10:38-42, we read of Martha welcoming Jesus as a guest in her home. Mary, her sister, sat at Jesus' feet and listened as He taught. Martha was distracted by the responsibilities of caring for her guests. When she asked Jesus to tell Mary to help her, Jesus replied, "Martha, Martha, you are worried and troubled about many things. But one thing is needed, and Mary has chosen that good part, which will not be taken away from her" (vv. 41-42).

It wasn't wrong or sinful for Martha to serve the guests she had invited into her home. Neither was it wrong for her to expect her sister Mary to help her. However, on this occasion, something more important was happening. God's Son was teaching. The best place for both of them to be was at His feet, paying attention to every word.

Life's choices are not always between right and wrong. Sometimes, they are in degrees of what is right or good. Paul's prayer for the Philippians was "that your love may abound still more and more in knowledge and all discernment, that you may approve the things that are excellent..." (Php. 1:9-10). Approving the things that are *excellent* requires us to know more than right and wrong. In some situations, we need to understand the difference between good, better, and best.

3. Christians Should Maintain Their Focus

Paul identified Demas as one of his fellow laborers (Philemon 24). However, just a few years later, Paul would lament, "For Demas has forsaken me, having loved this present world, and has departed for Thessalonica..." (2 Tim. 4:10). This trusted Christian had forsaken Paul because he loved the world more than he loved the Lord.

If the devil can't extinguish our zeal, he does the next best thing—he disables our steering and gets us sidetracked from our goal. Satan uses several successful tools to tamper with the steering of our spiritual lives.

- **The pleasures of this world**. Demas forsook the work of the gospel because he developed a love for this present world (2 Tim. 4:10). We are not to love the world or the things in the world (1 John 2:15-17).

  Paul warned that a love of money can cause some to stray from the faith and pierce themselves through with many sorrows (1 Tim 6:10). Nothing in this world is more valuable than your soul (Matt. 16:26), yet Satan temps many Christians to exchange their souls for sin's passing pleasures (Heb. 11:25).

To be "in the world but not of the world" presents a great challenge. Because Satan repeatedly tempts us with this world's allurements, we must constantly remind ourselves that we are sojourners and pilgrims here and conduct ourselves accordingly (1 Pet. 2:11).

- **Suffering and persecution**. If Satan can't get us to abandon our faith for sinful pleasure, he tries to discourage us with hardships. He used this tactic in an attempt to get Job to curse God to His face (Job 1:9-12; 2:3-7). In the Parable of the Sower, the seed sown on stony ground wilted under the heat of "tribulation and persecution" (Matt. 13:21).

  God equips us to withstand such adversarial efforts by warning us that they will come. "We must through many tribulations enter the kingdom of God" (Acts 14:22). A well-grounded faith helps us keep our focus on Jesus during the storms of life (Heb. 12:2; Col. 3:1-2).

- **Pride**. Satan is a master at using pride to redirect a Christian's zeal toward sin and destruction. Some people abandon the Lord and His church because of hurt feelings. Maybe someone at church mistreats them (intentionally or accidentally). Maybe they don't feel like they are being used or appreciated. The way to avoid this trap is to "let nothing be done through selfish ambition or conceit, but in lowliness of mind let each esteem others better than himself. Let each of you look out not only for his own interests, but also for the interests of others" (Php. 2:3-4).

Conclusion

A Christian who is on fire for the Lord should be "zealous for good works" (Titus 2:14). However, if his steering isn't working properly, the fired-up Christian can't maintain good works. It is important to have zeal for the Lord, but we need to make sure this zeal remains focused in the right direction.

Questions

1. What does Galatians 4:18 (NKJV) say about zeal? _____
   _____

2. In what ways are we to treat that which is evil and that which is good (Rom. 12:9)? _____
_____

3. How are we to discern good from evil? What standard did God give us (Psa. 119:160)? _____
_____

4. What should we be able to discern or distinguish if we have exercised our senses by studying God's word (Heb. 5:14)? _____
_____

5. What is Scripture able to do for us (2 Tim. 3:17)? _____
_____

6. Was it sinful for Martha to serve her guests (Luke 10:38-42)? On this occasion, what would have been the better choice? _____
_____

7. How did Satan redirect Demas' zeal (2 Tim. 4:10)? _____
_____

8. How are we to conduct ourselves in this world (1 Pet. 2:11)? _____
_____

9. How can we remain focused while we are going through times of suffering (Heb. 12:2; Col. 3:1-2)? _____
_____
_____

10. How does Satan use pride to get people to leave the Lord? _____
_____
_____

Protecting Our Zeal

Lesson 4

We likened zeal to fire in our previous lessons. Fire has great power, but it is also vulnerable. Numerous things can extinguish a fire. The same thing is true regarding our zeal for the Lord.

Satan is our enemy. He does not want us to be zealous for good works. He wants to extinguish our zeal.

We know how Satan works (2 Cor. 2:11). Deception is one of his most effective devices. We must guard against Satan's lies in every area of our lives; this includes protecting our zeal for the Lord. This lesson considers four different lies Satan tells us about zeal.

Lie Number 1 - "Zeal is Maintained by Focusing on What is New"

New things (a new baby, job, friends, etc.) often cause excitement. Some Christians get excited about new hymns, a new preacher, or a new approach to spreading the gospel. This excitement is sometimes mistaken for zeal.

The problem with excitement caused by new things is that it soon disappears. The only way to recapture this kind of excitement is by constantly pursuing new things. Such people are like the citizens of Athens. "For all the Athenians and the foreigners who were there spent their time in nothing else but either to tell or to hear some new thing" (Acts 17:21).

Thankfully, God provided an escape from the endless pursuit of new things. True zeal comes from understanding God's word and will for our lives. Our zeal for the Lord's work is *stirred up* when we are reminded of the truths in God's word (2 Peter 1:12-13), not when we are introduced to something new.

We maintain zeal for the Lord and remain on the right track when we are content to walk in the "old paths" (Jer. 6:16). There isn't necessarily anything wrong with new things, but pursuing new things is not the proper way to maintain zeal for the Lord.

Lie Number 2 – "Zeal is Measured by the Sins We Avoid"

Are you one of those Christians who defines *soundness* by the things you don't do?

- "I don't lie, steal, cheat, curse, gossip, drink, etc."
- "The church of which I am a member doesn't have a fellowship hall, athletic programs, or women preachers. We don't send money to orphan homes, colleges, or missionary societies."

Everything in life has balance. This is true of discipleship. There are sins to avoid, but it is equally important to do good works. Notice the two sides of James 1:27—pure and undefiled religion before God is based, not only on keeping ourselves unspotted from the world, but also on doing good to those in need.

Zeal is measured by activity—not inactivity (James 2:14-17). The church in Sardis was dead, and the church in Laodicea was lukewarm (Rev. 3:1-2, 15-16).

It is important to keep ourselves free from sin, but we must also actively participate in the Lord's work.

Lie Number 3 – "Zeal is Evaluated by Judging Others"

In the parable of the Pharisee and the Tax Collector (Luke 18:9-12), the self-righteous Pharisee gave himself a glowing review before God: "I am not like other men – extortioners, unjust, adulterers, or even as this tax collector. I fast twice a week; I give tithes of all that I possess." Because of his attitude, God rejected his prayer.

We can always find people worse than ourselves to use as comparisons for determining our zeal. This does not produce zeal. It produces a judgmental, condemning attitude toward others. This kind of attitude destroys zeal and good works.

Likewise, we can always find people who are doing more than we are. We can use these individuals to justify a negative critique of ourselves. We end up feeling worthless; our zeal is extinguished, and Satan has won the battle.

God's truth combats this lie. God wants us to judge ourselves by the standards in His Word, not by what others do. God made us as individuals. He knows our strengths, talents, and unique opportunities. He expects us to use them to His glory.

Lie Number 4 – "Zeal is Best at the Beginning"

Becoming a Christian brings true joy, excitement, and zeal.

- "And the multitudes with one accord heeded the things spoken by Philip, hearing and seeing the miracles which he did... And there was great joy in that city" (Acts 8:6, 8).
- "Now when they came up out of the water, the Spirit of the Lord caught Philip away, so that the eunuch saw him no more; and he went on his way rejoicing" (Acts 8:39).
- "And he took them the same hour of the night and washed their stripes. And immediately he and all his family were baptized. Now when he had brought them into his house, he set food before them; and he rejoiced, having believed in God with all his household" (Acts 16:33-34).

However, this initial excitement can diminish, and a Christian can feel that his zeal is gone. Growing and maturing in Christ brings challenges. Satan can tempt us to accept that "zeal naturally decreases over time."

This is a lie. The truth is that zeal can remain kindled with a "press on" attitude like that set forth by Paul in Philippians 3:12-15. Despite his increasing age (2 Tim. 4:6-8) and numerous discouraging experiences (2 Cor. 11:23-28), Paul's fire for the Lord never went out! Let's follow his example, which will be discussed in more detail in lessons 6 and 7.

Conclusion

Satan has always worked to destroy God's people through deception (John 8:44; Rev. 12:9). He wants us to believe his lies about zeal, but the truth of God's word counters and defeats these lies.

- Zeal is not based on what is new, but on what is true.
- Zeal is best measured, not by what we don't do, but by faithful obedience.
- Zeal is not determined by others, but by God's standards.
- Zeal can continue to burn hot throughout our lives if we protect it, fuel it, and press on in God's service.

Questions

1. What kinds of things can threaten or extinguish a fire? _____
   _____
   _____

2. What confidence does 2 Corinthians 2:11 give us for our ongoing battle with Satan? _____

3. What does Satan do to the whole world (Rev. 12:9)? _____

4. What was characteristic of the people in Athens (Acts 17:21)? _____

5. What important thing did Peter want to accomplish by writing his second epistle (2 Pet. 1:12-13)? _____

6. What complaint did the Lord have against the church in Sardis (Rev. 3:1-2)? _____

7. What complaint did the Lord have against the church in Laodicea (Rev. 3:15-16)? _____

8. What unwise practice did Paul avoid (2 Cor. 10:12)? _____

9. Why is it dangerous to compare ourselves to those who are worse than we are? _____

10. Why is it dangerous to compare ourselves to those who are better than we are? _____

11. What attitude did Paul commend in Philippians 3:12-14? _____

The Zeal of Jesus

Lesson 5

Zeal is "great energy or enthusiasm in pursuit of a cause or objective." In this study, we liken zeal to fire.

Isaiah spoke of Jesus as the Lord's Servant who "will not quarrel nor cry out" (Matt. 12:19; Isa. 42:1-3). Jesus described Himself as being *gentle and lowly in heart* (Matt. 11:29). However, this does not mean He wasn't on fire and full of zeal. Our Lord's life exhibited a burning zeal.

Jesus is our example and pattern to follow (1 Pet. 2:21). In lesson 5, we will consider two areas in which Jesus manifested His zeal.

Zeal for His Father's Work

In just three and a half years, Jesus accomplished the greatest work ever done. He preached the gospel of the kingdom throughout Galilee. He did mighty works that proved He was the Son of God. He trained the 12 apostles. He offered the perfect sacrifice for our sins. Jesus completed these amazing tasks because of His incredible work ethic, a work ethic driven by great zeal.

Jesus began at an early age. When He was 12 years old, His parents searched for and found Him in the temple, listening to the teachers and asking them questions. When questioned about this, Jesus responded, "Why did you seek Me? Did you not know that I must be about My Father's business?" (Luke 2:49).

Jesus' zeal is seen at the beginning of His earthly ministry (Mark 1:35-39). Knowing His days would be busy, He made it a habit to awaken early in the morning and find a secluded place to be alone with the Father in prayer. After preaching the gospel in one place, He made it His aim to go to other towns. "I must preach the kingdom of God to the other cities also, because for this purpose I have been sent" (Luke 4:43).

Statements Jesus made during His ministry reveal His zeal for the Father's work.

- "My food is to do the will of Him who sent Me, and to finish His work" (John 4:34). Jesus was hungry and tired when He encountered the Samaritan woman at the well (vv. 6, 8, 31-33). Despite these circumstances, He took time to initiate a life-changing conversation with her and help her come to a point of faith. He stirred up her zeal (vv. 28-29). Jesus came to finish the work the Father gave Him. The opportunity to reach this soul presented itself, and it wouldn't wait (v. 35). How many times have we allowed opportunities to slip by because they conflicted with our schedules?

- "I always do those things that please Him" (John 8:29). As our Lord's ministry grew, so did His conflicts with those who opposed Him. He knew enemies were plotting against Him and that such efforts would eventually end in His death. Despite what the Jewish leaders thought and said, Jesus never backed down. He made it His aim to always do the things that pleased His Father. "For I have come down from heaven, not to do My own will, but the will of Him who sent Me" (John 6:38). Are we always seeking to do the things that please God?

- "I must work the works of Him who sent Me while it is day; the night is coming when no one can work" (John 9:4). Jesus and His disciples were escaping some Jews who were seeking to stone Him when they encountered a man born blind (John 8:59-9:3). The disciples asked about the man's condition, and Jesus took the time to heal him. The Lord had a sense of urgency regarding the completion of His work. It had to be done because of the rapid approach of a time when no work could be done. Do we serve the Lord with a sense of urgency, or do we believe there will be plenty of time later?

- "It is finished!" (John 19:30). Jesus died at the age of 33. With His dying breath, He could honestly say He had fulfilled His purpose. He had completed His Father's will for His life. He worked right up to the very end. "I have glorified You on the earth. I have finished the work which You have given Me to do" (John 17:4). Most of us will probably leave this world knowing we could have done more to serve and glorify God. Will we be motivated by our Lord's example and work until the end?

Zeal for His Father's Honor (John 2:13-17)

At the time of Passover, Jesus went up to Jerusalem and saw the temple in an unacceptable condition. "And He found in the temple those who sold oxen and sheep and doves, and the money changers doing business" (v. 14). The temple's open courtyards resembled a sale barn and a flea market. Along with the oxen, sheep, and doves would be cages, pens, straw, and manure. The sight, sound, and smell of this irreverent commotion stoked our Lord's zeal.

Jesus did something uncharacteristic of the way we usually picture Him. He made a whip out of cords and began lashing it about at the people, driving them and their animals out of the temple. He overturned the tables that had been set up for business and poured out the money on the ground (v. 15). He gave the order, "Take these things away; stop making My Father's house a place of business" (v. 16, NASU).

Why did our Lord behave in this manner? These people were doing business in the place meant to honor God's presence. It was a sacred place set aside for prayer, worship, and spiritual service. They had turned it into a combination bank and stockyard.

While to us, this behavior appears to be *un-Christ-like*, John said that on this occasion, Jesus acted exactly how the Messiah should have acted. His reaction to this insulting behavior in His Father's temple fulfilled the prophecy in Psalm 69:9, "Because zeal for Your house has eaten me up."

Jesus was kind and gentle to those who were suffering. He was patient with those who were struggling. He was even willing to tolerate personal insults and injuries. However, He wouldn't tolerate such insults to His Father! Do we have this kind of zeal for God? While we may not have the authority to stop people from dishonoring Him, does it stir our zeal when people make fun of God or use His name in vain?

Conclusion

Jesus showed great zeal in His work. It was motivated by His love for the Father and commitment to finish His task. Jesus did not come to earth to be served as a King. He came on a rescue mission. "For the Son of Man has come to seek and to save that which was lost" (Luke 19:10). This work was urgent.

Jesus is our perfect example in all things. He shows us exactly how to please the Father. We need to develop Christ-like zeal for God's work and honor.

Questions

1. In your own words, describe the condition of the temple when Jesus arrived for Passover (John 2:14). _____

_____

2. How did Jesus react to this situation (vv. 15-16)? _____
   _____

3. Why did He react this way (v. 17)? _____
   _____

4. What priority did Jesus display at age 12 (Luke 2:49)? _____
   _____

5. What did Jesus identify as His "food" (John 4:34)? What did He mean?
   _____
   _____

6. What was Jesus' constant goal (John 8:29)? _____
   _____

7. Why did Jesus show urgency about doing His Father's work (John 9:4)?
   _____
   _____

8. According to John's gospel, what were our Lord's final words from the cross (John 19:30)? _____
   _____

9. How would you feel about Jesus calling on us to be "zealous for good works" (Titus 2:14) if He wasn't zealous for good works? ____
   _____
   _____

10. In what ways does our Lord's example challenge you to be more zealous for good works? _____
    _____
    _____

The Zeal of Paul – Part 1

Lesson 6

The English word *zeal* is defined as "great energy or enthusiasm in pursuit of a cause or objective." In our study, we liken zeal to the fire of a motor that propels a car.

If ever a man was on fire for the Lord, it was the apostle Paul. He called for all Christians to follow his example. "Brethren, join in following my example, and note those who so walk, as you have us for a pattern" (Php. 3:17). In lessons 6 and 7, we consider the role that zeal played in Paul's life and the ways we need to follow his example today.

Before His Conversion

Before he became the beloved apostle Paul, he was Saul of Tarsus (Acts 13:9). Saul was feared as a great enemy of the church. He zealously led persecutions against Christians (Php. 3:6).

> Galatians 1:13-14
> 13 For you have heard of my former conduct in Judaism, how I persecuted the church of God beyond measure and tried to destroy it.
> 14 And I advanced in Judaism beyond many of my contemporaries in my own nation, being more exceedingly *zealous* for the traditions of my fathers.
>
> Acts 22:3-5
> 3 I am indeed a Jew, born in Tarsus of Cilicia, but brought up in this city at the feet of Gamaliel, taught according to the strictness of our fathers' law, and was *zealous* toward God as you all are today.
> 4 I persecuted this Way to the death, binding and delivering into prisons both men and women,
> 5 as also the high priest bears me witness, and all the council of the elders, from whom I also received letters to the brethren, and went to Damascus to bring in chains even those who were there to Jerusalem to be punished.

Saul's desire to destroy the church evidenced his great zeal for God. His intense efforts were unmeasurable. He even traveled to foreign cities to arrest Christians and bring them back to Jerusalem to be punished. In his mind, Saul believed that, by destroying Christianity, he was doing God a great service (Acts 23:1).

Some would see Saul of Tarsus as an unlikely candidate for the gospel. Christians feared him and doubted his conversion (Acts 9:26). However, he had a great zeal for God. This was something of great value the Lord could use. Saul just needed someone to point him in the right direction (1 Tim. 1:13). After his conversion, the Lord used Saul to labor for the gospel with the same zeal and intensity with which he had previously persecuted it. "But they were hearing only, 'He who formerly persecuted us now preaches the faith which he once tried to destroy'" (Gal. 1:23).

There are others like Saul of Tarsus around us today. Don't write off people who are zealously involved in religious error. If their love for God's truth equals their zeal, they can be converted.

After His Conversion

Once he became a Christian and an apostle, Paul got to work channeling his zeal for God toward saving the lost.

The Lord appeared to Saul on the road to Damascus to call him to preach the gospel to both Jews and Gentiles. "Therefore, King Agrippa, I was not disobedient to the heavenly vision, but declared first to those in Damascus and in Jerusalem, and throughout all the region of Judea, and then to the Gentiles, that they should repent, turn to God, and do works befitting repentance" (Acts 26:19-20).

Although he was the apostle to the Gentiles, Paul had great zeal for the salvation of the Jews. "Brethren, my heart's desire and prayer to God for Israel is that they may be saved" (Rom. 10:1). However, he equally desired to save the Gentiles. "I am a debtor both to Greeks and to barbarians, both to wise and to unwise. So, as much as is in me, I am ready to preach the gospel to you who are in Rome also" (Rom. 1:14-15). This indebtedness was motivated, in part, by the fact that he had previously done much harm to the cause of Christ. It was also motivated by his calling to be an apostle. "For if I preach the gospel, I have nothing to boast of, for necessity is laid upon me; yes, woe is me if I do not preach the gospel!" (1 Cor. 9:16). Like the prophet Jeremiah, God's word burned like fire within Paul's heart (Jer. 20:9). He couldn't hold it back.

Paul's zeal to save lost souls drove him to travel great distances to preach. "And so I have made it my aim to preach the gospel, not where Christ was named, lest I should build on another man's foundation, but as it is written: 'To whom He was not announced, they shall see; and those who have not heard shall understand'" (Rom. 15:20-21). The book of Acts records Paul's preaching journeys. It is estimated that he traveled over 10,000 miles, on foot, to preach the gospel.

Paul labored tirelessly wherever he went. The opening statements of his address to the Ephesian elders give us a glimpse of Paul's local work (Acts 20:18-21).

- He saw himself as serving the Lord while laboring with a local church (v. 19; Col. 3:22-24).
- He willingly endured tears and trials when people opposed his work (v. 19).
- He taught everything that was needed and helpful (v. 20; 27).
- He took advantage of every opportunity, preaching publicly and teaching from house to house (v. 20).
- He taught everyone willing to listen (v. 21).

Paul never changed or compromised the gospel message. He had confidence in its power (Rom. 1:16) and taught the same thing everywhere he went (1 Cor. 4:17). However, he was willing to change his approach, depending on who he was teaching.

- When teaching *believers* (Jews and proselytes), he appealed to the Hebrew Scriptures. "Then Paul, as his custom was, went in to them, and for three Sabbaths reasoned with them from the Scriptures, explaining and demonstrating that the Christ had to suffer and rise again from the dead, and saying, 'This Jesus whom I preach to you is the Christ'" (Acts 17:2-3).

- When teaching *unbelievers* (Gentiles), he used a different approach. When preaching to the idol worshipers in Lystra, he pointed to God as the Creator and providential caretaker of all mankind (Acts 14:8-18). When preaching to the philosophers of Athens, he showed how the "unknown God" answered mankind's most basic questions (Acts 17:22-31).

Paul was willing to adapt his approach because his goal was to save souls. As best he could, he "became all things to all men, that I (he) might by all means save some" (1 Cor. 9:19-23).

Conclusion

No one can doubt or challenge Paul's zeal. He was filled with zeal for God before his conversion, and after learning the truth, he did everything he could to save others. This same zeal characterized more areas of Paul's life. We will consider them in the next lesson.

Questions

1. What evidence did Paul give to support his great zeal for God before his conversion (Gal. 1:13-14; Acts 22:3-5)? _____

2. Did he believe he was doing the right thing in these efforts (Acts 23:1)? _____

3. What reason did Paul give for his opposition to the gospel (1 Tim. 1:13)? _____

4. How did Paul react when Jesus called him to be an apostle (Acts 26:19-20)? _____

5. What was his heart's desire and prayer for Israel (Rom. 10:1)? _____

6. To whom did he feel indebted (Rom. 1:14)? _____

7. What was Paul's attitude toward preaching the gospel (1 Cor. 9:16; Jer. 20:9)? _____

8. What goal motivated him to travel to new places to preach the gospel (Rom. 15:20-21)? _____

9. What do we learn about Paul's local work from Acts 20:18-21? _____

10. Why did he use a different approach when preaching to different kinds of people (1 Cor. 9:22)? _____

The Zeal of Paul – Part 2

Lesson 7

In the previous lesson, we began our look at examples of zeal in the apostle Paul's life. He encouraged the Corinthians to "imitate me, just as I also imitate Christ" (1 Cor. 11:1). As Jesus had been zealous about His Father's work, so had Paul. He left behind an example and pattern for all Christians to follow (Php. 3:17).

In this lesson, we consider Paul's zeal for Christians and the Lord's church.

Zeal in Strengthening Christians

Paul did not achieve his evangelistic goals by just getting prospects into the water. His work did not end at their baptism. Paul was faithful to every part of the Great Commission. "Go therefore and make disciples of all the nations, baptizing them in the name of the Father and of the Son and of the Holy Spirit, *teaching them to observe all things that I have commanded you*, and lo, I am with you always, even to the end of the age" (Matt. 28:19-20, emphasis mine – HR). The goal was to bring the gospel to every lost person and then bring every saved person to spiritual maturity in Christ.

On Paul's first preaching journey, after he and Barnabas had made many disciples in Derbe, they could have continued their journey and eventually returned to their home congregation in Antioch of Syria. Instead, "they returned to Lystra, Iconium, and Antioch, strengthening the souls of the disciples, exhorting them to continue in the faith, and saying, 'We must through many tribulations enter the kingdom of God.' So when they had appointed elders in every church, and prayed with fasting, they commended them to the Lord in whom they had believed" (Acts 14:21-23). Before leaving the area, they made sure these new Christians had the strength, encouragement, and organization they needed to survive.

In many of Paul's epistles to Christians, he expressed great concern for their spiritual progress and well-being.

- Galatians was an emergency letter written to churches being infiltrated by Judaizing teachers who were seducing Gentile Christians away from the gospel's purity. They had to stop following this error or forfeit their souls (Gal. 1:6-9; 3:1; 5:1-4). Paul was not willing to give up on the Galatians. Instead, he wrote, "My little children, for whom I am again in the anguish of childbirth until Christ is formed in you!" (Gal. 4:19, ESV).

Paul compared his initial labors and trials among the Galatians to the labor pains endured by a mother giving birth. He continued this *anguish of childbirth* until they developed to the point of spiritual maturity. Christ would be *formed* in them when their minds were renewed with the thinking and will of the Lord (Rom. 12:2; Eph. 4:23).

- The Colossian letter was written to a church being troubled by various kinds of error. Paul wrote, "For I want you to know what a great conflict I have for you and those in Laodicea, and for as many as have not seen my face in the flesh" (Col. 2:1). The word *conflict* is from the Greek word *agon*. This term describes the dedication and effort exerted by athletes, runners, and charioteers competing in the arena. In a spiritual context, it is "any struggle with dangers, annoyances, obstacles, standing in the way of faith, holiness, and a desire to spread the gospel" (Thayer 10).

Paul exhibited his zeal by his willingness to go through any obstacle to achieve his goal—strengthening Christians. Some of these obstacles are listed in 2 Corinthians 11:23-28.

> 23 Are they ministers of Christ?—I speak as a fool—I am more: in labors more abundant, in stripes above measure, in prisons more frequently, in deaths often.
> 24 From the Jews five times I received forty stripes minus one.
> 25 Three times I was beaten with rods; once I was stoned; three times I was shipwrecked; a night and a day I have been in the deep;
> 26 in journeys often, in perils of waters, in perils of robbers, in perils of my own countrymen, in perils of the Gentiles, in perils in the city, in perils in the wilderness, in perils in the sea, in perils among false brethren;
> 27 in weariness and toil, in sleeplessness often, in hunger and thirst, in fastings often, in cold and nakedness —
> 28 besides the other things, what comes upon me daily: my deep concern for all the churches.

- First Thessalonians was written to a young and troubled church. Paul had to leave these disciples before he had time to establish them in their new faith (see Acts 17:1-10). He had tried to return, but was unable to do so (1 Thess. 2:17-20). "Therefore, when we could no longer endure it, we thought it good to be left in Athens alone, and sent Timothy, our brother and minister of God, and our fellow laborer in the gospel of Christ, to establish you and encourage you concerning your faith" (3:1-2). Paul was willing to be without his trusted coworker to make sure the faith of these young Christians was not shaken and destroyed.

If we had this same zeal for strengthening Christians, perhaps there would be stronger churches and fewer members leaving the Lord.

Zeal in Protecting the Church

As an apostle, Paul had an additional charge and challenge—protecting the church against error and apostasy. To the Corinthians, he wrote, "For I am jealous for you with godly jealousy. For I have betrothed you to one husband, that I may present you as a chaste virgin to Christ" (2 Cor. 11:2). The words *jealous* and *jealousy* are translated from *zeloo* and *zelos* (the same words translated as *zealous* and *zeal* in the New Testament).

Instead of a mother laboring in pain to give birth, Paul here pictured himself as a father burdened with the responsibility of keeping his children pure until marriage.

> "These words express his emotions as a concerned father, whose responsibility is to guard the Corinthians' purity and fidelity until Christ returns for his bride. Moreover, he describes the engagement period in terms of Jewish marriage laws: the betrothal is an event in the past whereas the marriage is an event that will occur at sometime in the future and sometimes even the distant future... Paul assumes the place of a father whose duty is to assure the chastity of his daughter during the betrothal period" (Curry 342).

We are not apostles, but we do bear responsibility for protecting the doctrinal and spiritual purity of the local churches where we are members. This starts with keeping ourselves pure. We must also make sure we zealously and faithfully follow the Lord's commands regarding sin in the local church (Matt. 18:15-17; 1 Cor. 5; 2 Thess. 3:6-15).

Conclusion

Paul faced numerous obstacles in his efforts to serve the Lord, but he never lost his zeal. It continued as long as he lived. "I have fought the good fight, I have finished the race, I have kept the faith. Finally, there is laid up for me the crown of righteousness, which the Lord, the righteous Judge, will give to me on that Day, and not to me only but also to all who have loved His appearing" (2 Tim. 4:7-8). Let us follow his example.

References

Curry, Melvin, "Truth Commentaries, the Book of 2 Corinthians," Bowling Green, Kentucky, Guardian of Truth Foundation, 2008, print.
Thayer, Joseph H., "Thayer's Greek-English Lexicon of the New Testament," Peabody, Massachusetts, Hendrickson Publishers, 1996, print.

Questions

1. According to the Great Commission, what were the apostles to do after they had made disciples (Matt. 28:20)? _____
   _____

2. What did Paul and Barnabas do for the young disciples in Lystra, Iconium, and Antioch (Acts 14:21-23)? _____
   _____
   _____

3. To what end did Paul labor as a mother, giving birth to a child (Gal. 4:19)? _____
   _____

4. How would Christ be formed in them (Rom. 12:2; Eph. 4:23)? _____
   _____

5. Colossians 2:1 uses the Greek word *agon*. From our lesson, explain how this word calls for one to show zeal. _____
   _____

6. Describe the extent of Paul's concern for the spiritual welfare of the Thessalonians (1 Thess. 2:17-3:2). _____
   _____

7. What responsibility did Paul accept regarding the spiritual and doctrinal purity of the church in Corinth (2 Cor. 11:2)? _____
   _____

8. What are some things we must do to keep ourselves doctrinally and morally pure? _____
   _____
   _____

9. What can happen if we are not zealous about keeping the local church pure? _____
   _____

10. How did Paul express the zeal of his final days (2 Tim. 4:7)? _____
   _____
   _____

Spreading the Gospel

Lesson 8

"The fruit of the righteous is a tree of life, and he who wins souls is wise" (Prov. 11:30). Trying to save those who are lost is a very good work. We can find modern churches that enjoy success and growth. They employ numerous gimmicks to attract and retain large crowds. Our standard must continue to be the example set by the New Testament church. When it comes to the work of evangelism, these disciples are worthy of our examination and imitation.

The church we read of in the book of Acts grew at a rate unheard of today. It started with only 120 people (Acts 1:15). On the Day of Pentecost, 3,000 people were added to the 120 (2:41). The number soon grew to include 5,000 men (4:4). This figure does not include the women.

By Acts 5, Luke stopped giving numerical figures and simply chronicled the church's incredible growth.

- "And believers were *increasingly added* to the Lord, *multitudes* of both men and women" (5:14).
- "Then the word of God spread, and the number of the disciples *multiplied greatly* in Jerusalem, and a great many of the priests were obedient to the faith" (6:7).
- "Then the churches throughout all Judea, Galilee, and Samaria had peace and were edified. And walking in the fear of the Lord and in the comfort of the Holy Spirit, they were *multiplied*" (9:31).
- "And the hand of the Lord was with them, and a *great number* believed and turned to the Lord... And a *great many people* were added to the Lord" (11:21, 24).
- "So the churches were strengthened in the faith, and *increased in number daily*" (16:5).

What caused this incredible growth? How can we hope to replicate it? No doubt, the Holy Spirit's miraculous work contributed to this amazing spread of the gospel. And these Christians were living in a unique time in history (Gal. 4:4). In that day, many hearts were ready to hear and respond to the gospel.

We can do nothing about these factors. The Holy Spirit's miraculous gifts have served their purposes and are no longer available to us. We can't change the time during which we live. However, another vitally important element was essential to this early church growth – individual Christians zealously spread the gospel. "Therefore those who were scattered went everywhere preaching the word" (Acts 8:4).

What generates in a Christian a passion and fire to be personally involved in spreading the gospel to the lost?

1. Love for the Lord

"If you love Me, keep My commandments" (John 14:15). If we love the Lord, we will do what He tells us to do—obey His word and carry out His wishes. Disciples are supposed to make disciples. The last command Jesus gave instructed His followers to observe all His commandments, including the command to go and make disciples (Matt. 28:19-20).

2. Our Lord's Example

"For the Son of Man has come to seek and to save that which was lost" (Luke 19:10). One's motive for seeking and saving the lost needs to go deeper than surface obedience to the Lord. Disciples need to follow their master's example. We need to be involved in doing what He did. Jesus actively sought the lost in order to save them.

3. Examples Set by Other Christians

Paul said Christians were motivated by his efforts to become "much more bold to speak the word without fear" (Php. 1:12-14). Energy, dedication, and enthusiasm are contagious. Seeing other Christians involved in good works and experiencing success in those works encourages us to do the same sort of work.

News of conversions in other places does not cause mature Christians to be envious or skeptical. It does not cause them to downplay their own abilities. Instead, it encourages them to become more involved in spreading the gospel.

4. Love for Lost Souls

Jesus tried to get His disciples to see the true spiritual condition of those around them. People are lost in sin and destined for eternal punishment in hell (Matt. 9:36-38). Evangelism is a good work because it is a rescue mission, and too few are involved in this work.

Most of us would do anything we could to save another person's physical life. If we happened to arrive at the scene of an emergency, we would act. We would speak up if we knew someone's life or health was in danger. Why do we remain silent when it comes to that same person's spiritual condition?

5. A Desire to Share Our Greatest Blessing

Andrew was one of the first disciples to meet Jesus (John 1:38-42). He was not content to enjoy this blessing alone. He found his brother and brought him to the Lord.

People around us desperately need Jesus! They may not realize it or care, but they need Him. We have found our greatest blessing—our Savior. We should want to share this great news with everyone.

6. A Moral Obligation

In 2 Kings 7:3-9, we read of four lepers who found their salvation. The Syrian army had abandoned their camp and left behind more food, wealth, and clothing than the lepers could ever use. As they were celebrating their discovery, they came to a realization. "Then they said to one another, 'We are not doing right. This day is a day of good news, and we remain silent. If we wait until morning light, some punishment will come upon us. Now therefore, come, let us go and tell the king's household'" (v. 9).

Nearby, there was a city full of people who were starving to death. It was not right for the lepers to keep the good news to themselves. In fact, they feared punishment for doing so. They went to the city and shared what they had found.

It is not right for us to keep the Gospel's good news to ourselves while so many around us are living and dying in sin. We will give account to God for our lives (2 Cor. 5:10), including our willingness to share the gospel with others.

Conclusion

The most successful evangelistic effort in history happened because individuals were personally involved in sharing the gospel. We live in a different time but have the same gospel, and the fields around us are just as white for harvest. We've considered numerous motivations to get involved in this good work. Pick one—and get busy!

Questions

1. What important factor in the growth of the first-century church can be replicated today (Acts 8:4)? _____
_____

2. How can our love for the Lord motivate us to try to convert people to Christ (John 14:15; Matt. 28:19-20)? _____
_____

3. How did Jesus describe His earthly mission (Luke 19:10)? _____
_____

4. What did Jesus train His apostles to do (Matt. 4:19)? _____
_____

5. How did some Christians react (what did they do) when they heard of Paul's struggles to spread the gospel (Php. 1:14)? _____
_____

6. How should we react when we hear of successful evangelistic efforts by other Christians or local congregations? _____
_____

7. What did Jesus say about the harvest of lost souls and the availability of laborers for this harvest (Matt. 9:36-38; John 4:35)? _____
_____

8. What was the first thing Andrew and Philip did when they found Jesus (John 1:35-46)? Why? _____
_____

9. Why did the four lepers tell others about the food they had found (2 Kings 7:9)? _____
_____

10. Can you think of other things that should motivate Christians to be zealous about saving the lost? _____
_____
_____

Encouraging Others

Lesson 9

Paul admonished the Thessalonians, "Therefore encourage one another and build one another up, just as you are doing" (1 Thess. 5:11, ESV). He gave this admonition to remind them that our Lord will return (v. 9). We don't know when, but He will "come like a thief in the night." However, if we aren't watching and prepared, we will receive God's wrath instead of the salvation of our souls.

Because of the certainty of this event, we are to "encourage one another." The word *encourage* is translated from the Greek word *parakaleo,* which means "a calling to one's side" (Vine 110) for exhortation, consolation, or comfort.

When we come to another person's side, we are to build up that person. Other translations say we are to "edify one another." This is translated from the Greek word *oikodomeo,* which means "promoting the spiritual growth and development of the character of believers, by teaching or by example, suggesting such spiritual progress as the result of patient labor" (Vine 194).

The Lord gave the local church three works: evangelism, edification, and benevolence. All three are important. In the previous lesson, we noted that individual members of the early church showed great zeal for the good work of evangelism. These same Christians were also committed to doing the good work of edifying or building up one another.

This work started immediately (Acts 2:42) and continued to be emphasized as the gospel spread. In his address to the elders of the church in Ephesus, Paul said, "So now, brethren, I commend you to God and to the word of His grace, which is able to build you up and give you an inheritance among all those who are sanctified" (Acts 20:32).

Barnabas

The book of Acts singles out Barnabas as one who was zealous in doing the good work of encouraging and edifying others.

1. He stood out to the apostles. "And Joses, who was also named Barnabas by the apostles (which is translated Son of Encouragement), a Levite of the country of Cyprus" (Acts 4:36). They gave him the name "Son of Encouragement." His ability to encourage others made him stand out in a congregation of over 3,000 people.

2. He encouraged congregations. The apostles sent Barnabas to the young church in Antioch of Syria. "When he came and had seen the grace of God, he was glad, and encouraged them all that with purpose of heart they should continue with the Lord" (Acts 11:23). While traveling with Paul, he encouraged the churches in Lystra, Iconium, and Antioch of Pisidia (Acts 14:21-22). This encouragement was likely done primarily through *preaching and teaching* God's word.

3. He encouraged individuals. Barnabas didn't limit his good works to public opportunities. He gladly encouraged and built up individual Christians when he had the opportunity. Luke wrote of his successful efforts to encourage Paul (Acts 9:26-27) and John Mark (Acts 15:36-39). These efforts were not done through preaching but by *going to the side of one* and giving them help.

Ways We Can Involve Ourselves in the Good Work of Encouraging Others

1. Set the proper example. Encouraging others begins with the simple step of living right before others. We can't influence others to do right by disappointing them with our ungodly behavior.

2. Offer words of praise. "Pleasant words are like a honeycomb, sweetness to the soul and health to the bones" (Prov. 16:24). People need to hear that they are appreciated and doing well. Offer sincere words of praise for the efforts and improvements shown by others. Be specific when praising those who lead in the worship services, preach, or teach Bible classes. "I appreciate that point you made in your sermon," "I'm glad you led that hymn," etc.

Praise the efforts of brethren who invite others to services and/or open their homes for get-togethers and Bible studies. These good works are difficult and often come with disappointments. A word of praise may help more than you realize.

Encourage teenagers and college students. They face incredible challenges and may be battling strong temptations. Instead of standing on the sidelines and lamenting the fact that many churches are losing their young people, be one who steps forward and encourages them to live for the Lord.

Praise young parents who struggle with their children during the worship services. Encourage those who are middle-aged. Appreciate those who are older. Every stage of life comes with unique challenges. Understand this fact and be a Barnabas to *everyone* you meet.

3. Help other Christians grow spiritually. Teaching a Bible Class is an obvious way to be involved in the work of edification. However, to some, the thought of teaching a class can be overwhelming. Instead of taking on a class for an entire quarter, volunteer to be a fill-in teacher or a helper to another member who is teaching a class. This is a great way to get started as a teacher.

   Take time to study with one who is young in the faith. I benefitted greatly when individual members took the time to answer my questions and help me better understand the Scriptures.

   Preachers and elders are to teach younger men how to teach God's word properly and effectively. "And the things that you have heard from me among many witnesses, commit these to faithful men who will be able to teach others also" (2 Tim. 2:2). Young men need help learning how to give invitations, prepare sermons, lead singing, lead prayers, and make comments at the Lord's table. This requires very little instruction time, but it helps develop those who will be edifying the Lord's church for years into the future.

4. Exhibit interest in those who appear to be overlooked, left out, or discouraged. Don't let brethren fall through the cracks. We are all different, and we have different needs. "Now we exhort you, brethren, warn those who are unruly, comfort the fainthearted, uphold the weak, be patient with all" (1 Thess. 5:14). While some brethren are, by nature, introverts and prefer to be left alone, others may be growing weak and starting to go astray. Try to be a person in the congregation with whom they can make a meaningful connection.

Conclusion

God, in His wisdom, did not intend for His saved people to live as mavericks and nomads. He joined us together into one body in His Son. We need each other. Let us follow the early church's example and be zealous about encouraging and building up one another.

References

Vine, W.E., Merrill F. Unger, and William White, Jr. Vine's Complete Expository Dictionary of Old and New Testament Words, Nashville, TN; Thomas Nelson Inc., 1985. Print.

Questions

1. What two-part admonition did Paul give in 1 Thessalonians 5:11? ____
   _____
   _____

2. What does it mean to encourage others? What action is involved in the Greek word *parakaleo*? _____
   _____
   _____

3. What kind of growth and progress was Paul interested in when he used the Greek word *oikodomeo*? _____
   _____

4. What is God's word able to do (Acts 20:32)? _____
   _____

5. How did Barnabas get his name? What trait of his stood out to the apostles (Acts 4:36)? _____
   _____

6. How did Barnabas and Paul encourage the disciples in Lystra, Iconium, and Antioch (Acts 14:21-22)? _____
   _____

7. How can a bad example be discouraging to other Christians? _____
   _____
   _____

8. What can you do to encourage members of your local congregation? __
   _____
   _____

9. How can you help other Christians grow spiritually? _____
   _____
   _____

10. What can you do to help Christians who are feeling left out or ignored?
_____
_____
_____

Helping Those in Need

Lesson 10

The title of our study comes from the book of Titus. "Who gave Himself for us, that He might redeem us from every lawless deed and purify for Himself His own special people, zealous for good works" (Titus 2:14). This epistle was written about a people who greatly needed this admonition.

Paul left the young evangelist Titus on the island of Crete (Titus 1:5). This island's inhabitants were notorious for being "liars, evil beasts, and lazy gluttons" (v. 12). The Christians on Crete had to break away from this way of life they had inherited from their ancestors and learned from their surroundings. Throughout the remainder of the epistle, Paul emphasized being *zealous for good works*.

- "...be a pattern of *good works*" (Titus 2:7).
- "Remind them...to be ready for every *good work*" (Titus 3:1).
- "This is a faithful saying, and these things I want you to affirm constantly, that those who have believed in God should be careful to maintain *good works*. These things are good and profitable to men" (3:8).
- "And let our people also learn to maintain *good works*, to meet urgent needs, that they may not be unfruitful" (3:14).

The Early Church

Along with evangelism and edification, benevolence was another good work carried out by local churches. The New Testament presents a pattern of individual Christians and local churches helping needy Christians.

From the very beginning of the church, members sacrificed and shared to help other members who were in need (Acts 2:44-45). It is important to note that the gospel did not call for Christians to establish a type of eutopia in which everyone's wealth was surrendered and shared equally. Individual Christians had God's permission to keep their money and use it as they pleased (Acts 5:1-4). Many of the new Christians in Acts 2 were converted while visiting Jerusalem for the Passover and Pentecost feast days (Acts 2:5). They had brought only enough funds to get them through these days and back home. After obeying the gospel, they chose to remain in Jerusalem. Their funds ran out, and they were in need. Other Christians shared with them so they could stay in Jerusalem and continue to learn from the apostles.

As the church grew, so did the number of needy members. However, generous Christians continued to sacrifice to meet this need. "Nor was there anyone among them who lacked; for all who were possessors of lands or houses sold them, and brought the proceeds of the things that were sold, and laid them at the apostles' feet; and they distributed to each as anyone had need" (Acts 4:34-35). The church soon appointed seven men to administer the daily distribution to the needy widows among their number (Acts 6:1-6).

Eventually, the gospel spread outside Judea and churches were established in other places. These churches were also involved in the good work of helping needy brethren in Judea. In Antioch of Syria, "the disciples, each according to his ability, determined to send relief to the brethren dwelling in Judea" (Acts 11:29). While on his third missionary journey, Paul was collecting funds from the Gentile churches to send to "the poor among the saints who are in Jerusalem" (Rom. 15:26). He spoke of this collection in 1 Corinthians 16:1-2 and 2 Corinthians 8-9.

It is important to notice two things about these benevolent efforts.

- First, these funds were always limited to needy saints. While individual Christians are free to use their personal funds to help non-Christians, the church does not have the authority to take money from its treasury to help everyone who is poor or in need. The divine pattern is that the church helps needy saints (Rom. 15:26). The local church can help Christian widows who have no family to care for them (1 Tim. 5:3-16; Acts 6:1-6).

- Second, churches sent the funds directly to those in need. No local church set itself up as a clearing house to expedite the flow of the collected funds. Money was not given to a separate organization that oversaw the work of helping needy Christians. Churches today can help Christians in need, but they must do so by sending the funds directly to those churches or members who are in need.

The instructions Paul emphasized in his letter to Titus are consistent with the church's practice from its very beginning. Christians who are saved by God's mercy and grace must be zealous to do good works.

Individual Christians

Other lessons in this workbook discuss in detail the specific works of spreading the gospel, edifying brethren, praying for others, and helping the sick. Following are some other things individual Christians can do to help those in need.

1. Provide food and clothing. These are basic human needs. Christians are to be watchful and willing to help during times of need. "If a brother or sister is naked and destitute of daily food, and one of you says to them, 'Depart in peace, be warmed and filled,' but you do not give them the things which are needed for the body, what does it profit?" (James 2:15-16). "But whoever has this world's goods, and sees his brother in need, and shuts up his heart from him, how does the love of God abide in him?" (1 John 3:17).

   The New Testament has no record of a local church operating a food pantry or comparable relief program for the community. Individual Christians are to fulfill such responsibilities as they have opportunity (Gal. 6:10). The Bible memorializes Dorcas as a good woman who helped others by making clothing for them (Acts 9:36-39). Christians today follow her example when they make or buy these basic needs for others.

2. Help the helpless. "Pure and undefiled religion before God and the Father is this: to visit orphans and widows in their trouble, and to keep oneself unspotted from the world" (James 1:27). The word *visit* does not mean to stop by and chat for a few minutes. It means to look upon and help. Government benevolent programs did not exist in the first century. *Orphans and widows* represent individuals who need help. Numerous Christians have become foster parents or have adopted children to provide the kind of help called for in this passage. Not every Christian can take on these tasks, but we are grateful for those who have and will.

3. Hospitality. Christians are to "be hospitable to one another without grumbling" (1 Pet. 4:9, c.f. Rom. 12:13). We think of hospitality as opening our homes to friends for a meal. However, the Greek term refers to a love for strangers (Heb. 13:2). Providing shelter to those who need a place to stay is a good work.

4. Other Works. There are many things we can do to help others.
   - Cleaning house, doing yard work, or shoveling a driveway.
   - Helping with auto maintenance or home repair.
   - Helping someone who is out of town (housesitting, getting their mail, feeding their pets, etc.).
   - Sharing produce or flowers from your garden.
   - Watching a young couple's children.
   - Giving rides to appointments, airport, etc.
   - Assisting those who are caring for loved ones.
   - Helping those who are moving away from or into your area.
   - Helping people find legal or financial help.

Conclusion

Christians are richly blessed in many ways. We have every spiritual blessing offered through Christ (Eph. 1:3-14) and a world-wide family of spiritual brothers and sisters. Most of us have an abundance of physical blessings. The Lord is watching to see how well we are sharing these blessings with others (Matt. 25:34-40). Let's do so with zeal.

Questions

1. What was the notorious character of the inhabitants of the island of Crete (Titus 1:12)? _____
   _____

2. Why did the early Christians sell their possessions and property and give the proceeds to others (Acts 2:44-45; 4:34-35)? _____
   _____

3. Describe the circumstances that caused the great need among some in the early church (Acts 2:5). _____
   _____

4. Does the gospel require Christians to sell their possessions and share the proceeds equally with all believers (Acts 5:4)? _____
   _____

5. Church benevolence has its limitations. Who is the church authorized to help from its treasury (Acts 11:29; Rom. 15:26)? _____
   _____

6. How did local churches convey their funds to those in need? _____
   _____
   _____

7. Does the local church have the authority to operate a food pantry for the members or community? Why or why not? _____
   _____
   _____

8. For what good work is Dorcas remembered (Acts 9:36-39)? _____

9. How does the Biblical idea of hospitality differ from our modern-day understanding and practice? _____

10. Does Jesus care if we are zealous for good works (Matt. 25:34-46)? ___

11. This lesson lists many good works. Can you think of other good works Christians should be ready to do? _____

Singing

Lesson 11

Zeal is the Christian's fire. When we stir up this fire in one another, the result is love and good works (Heb. 10:24). One of the easiest things we can do to stir up this fire is to encourage others by singing. "Let the word of Christ dwell in you richly in all wisdom, teaching and admonishing one another in psalms and hymns and spiritual songs, singing with grace in your hearts to the Lord" (Col. 3:16).

We Offer Our Singing to God

People sing for different reasons. However, when we are in our worship assemblies, we sing to offer praise to God. Paul instructed us to sing with grace in our hearts *to the Lord.* Sometimes, the people in the pews during a worship assembly are referred to as *the audience.* This is unfortunate and inaccurate. God is the audience! We offer worship to Him.

Congregational singing is also a spiritual sacrifice. "Therefore by Him let us continually offer the sacrifice of praise to God, that is, the fruit of our lips, giving thanks to His name" (Heb. 13:15). When it comes to sacrifices, God accepts only the best. Therefore, we must do our best when we sing. Not every Christian is blessed with a pleasing singing voice, but we are to do the best we can as we make melody in our hearts to the Lord (Eph. 5:19).

We Sing for One Another

The fact that a single act of worship can accomplish more than one thing exhibits God's wisdom. Singing is a bi-directional activity. God designed it to be of benefit, not only to ourselves but also to other worshipers. Congregational singing is not a performance for the people, but it is a means of edifying the church.

Paul spoke of singing as a means of *teaching.* As we sing during worship, we educate (instruct) one another. Christians need continual teaching (Heb. 5:12). Our hearts need to be stirred up by way of reminders (2 Pet. 1:12-13). This stirring up of zeal in one another can happen in numerous ways and at various times. One of these is singing.

Singing is also a means of *admonishing* one another. The word *admonishing* is translated from the Greek term *nouthetountes,* which "denotes guidance or counsel concerning improper conduct, and thus means to warn others in order to help them improve their spiritual lives" (Olbricht 380). We all need to be reminded, warned, reproved, and motivated to live better spiritual lives. Congregational singing helps meet this need.

Requirements

Mutual edification through singing does not happen accidentally or automatically. Some things are necessary for our singing to teach and admonish one another.

1. We must be present. We can't teach and admonish one another with our singing if we aren't present when and where the singing is taking place. We can certainly benefit from watching a recorded or livestream worship service, but doing so does not allow us to teach and admonish one another. One who watches a livestream service because he doesn't want to physically assemble is forsaking the assembling of the saints (Heb. 10:25).

2. We must participate. Just being present in a room where worship is taking place doesn't necessarily mean we are worshiping. "These people draw near to Me with their mouth, and honor Me with their lips, but their heart is far from Me" (Matt. 15:8). It is a good thing to assemble with Christians who are worshiping God in spirit and truth, but we must open our mouths and sing.

3. The songs must be scriptural. We are not authorized to sing whatever we want to sing. Just as the preacher is limited to the proper source material (the Bible), song leaders are also limited to the types of songs to be sung in worship. Paul specified *psalms, hymns, and spiritual songs*.
    - A *psalm* is an inspired song. The Old Testament book of Psalms contains 150 of these songs. Many of the songs we sing in worship today are patterned after psalms.
    - A *hymn* is a non-inspired song of praise that addresses God or is about God.
    - *Spiritual songs* are spiritually themed songs designed to teach, warn, or encourage obedience.

4. We must understand the songs. When he instructed the Corinthians regarding their worship assemblies, Paul said he was careful to "sing with the understanding" (1 Cor. 14:15). A song's melody or meter may entertain and emotionally move us. Still, we can't be edified, taught, or admonished if we don't understand the words.

    Songs are poetry, which often employs figurative or symbolic language. Our hymns contain words or phrases that some may not understand.
    - "Night, with ebon pinion..."
    - "Here I raise my Ebenezer..."

- "In vain in high and holy lays..."
- "Sharon's perfect sweet rose..."
- "O Lord, prepare me to be a sanctuary..."
- "High above the seraphim..."
- "A bulwark never failing..."

Some songs require explanations to make sure we all understand what we are singing. A song leader does the congregation a favor when he gives such explanations before leading songs containing words and phrases that are no longer part of our common vernacular.

Conclusion

Congregational singing is an important part of worship. We don't sing to connect the other acts of worship (prayer, the sermon, communion, and taking up the collection). Our singing is a spiritual sacrifice each of us offers to God. It is a means of teaching and admonishing our brethren and stirring up one another to love and good works. As such, singing psalms, hymns, and spiritual songs is a good work we should be zealous to perform.

References

Olbricht, Owen D. Truth for Today Commentary, Colossians and Philemon, Searcy, AR; Resource Publications, 2005. Print.

Questions

1. Why shouldn't we refer to worshipers in the pew as the audience? _____

2. How is our praise a sacrifice offered to God (Heb. 13:15; Eph. 5:19)? ___

3. What quality of sacrifices will God accept? _____

4. Does this mean those who can't sing well shouldn't sing? Why or why not? _____

5. How do we teach one another when we sing? _____

6. What does it mean to admonish one another, and how do we accomplish this task by singing? _____

7. Is it possible to be present where worship is taking place and still not worship (Matt. 15:8)? _____

8. What three types of songs are we authorized to sing in worship to God (Col. 3:16)? _____

9. What two requirements for our singing are found in 1 Corinthians 14:15? _____

Praying

Lesson 12

Offering prayers to God is a good and important work every Christian can do. We need to do this good work with zeal.

Paul told the Colossians to "continue earnestly in prayer, being vigilant in it with thanksgiving" (Col. 4:2). "Continue earnestly" is translated from the Greek word *proskartereo,* which means to be diligent or to constantly attend to a person or a thing. The same Greek word is used in Romans 12:12 ("...continuing steadfastly in prayer"). To be "vigilant" in prayer is to remain alert and active. As Paul wrote in another epistle, we are to "pray without ceasing" (1 Thess. 5:17).

James said, "The effective, fervent prayer of a righteous man avails much" (James 5:16b). This verse promises that our prayers have great power; they accomplish, or avail, much. However, there are conditions. First, prayer must be offered by a righteous person. Second, prayers must be effective and fervent.

The words "effective, fervent" in the New King James Version are translated from the Greek word *energeo,* which is the root of our English word "energy." *Energeo* means to be active or to put forth power. Our prayers have great power, but only if we put our energy (zeal) into them.

Prayer is an important part of the Christian's life. It should not be neglected. Neither should it become a mindless routine. It requires energy, diligence, and vigilance. In other words, it requires zeal.

Early Church Examples

The early Christians were zealous and devoted to the practice of prayer. They left us a worthy example to follow.

1. In the ten days between the Lord's ascension and Pentecost, the apostles "continued with one accord in prayer and supplication, with the women and Mary the mother of Jesus, and with His brothers" (Acts 1:14). Jesus had told them to go to Jerusalem and wait (v. 4). What should we do when we don't know what to do? We should pray.

2. The newborn church was devoted to prayer. "And they continued steadfastly in the apostles' doctrine and fellowship, in the breaking of bread, and in prayers" (Acts 2:42).

3. In the face of opposition, the apostles prayed together. The Jewish leaders threatened Peter and John and commanded them not to speak or teach in the name of Jesus (Acts 4:18-21). Peter and John repeated these words to the rest of the apostles, and together, they prayed to God for boldness to continue speaking His word (vv. 23-31). We should pray when we face threats and opposition to our efforts to serve God faithfully.

4. The apostles engaged in continual prayer. They ensured the appointment of capable men to oversee the work of benevolence so they could give themselves "continually to prayer and to the ministry of the word" (Acts 6:4).

5. In Acts 12, Herod had the apostle James put to death. He then arrested Peter who, no doubt, awaited the same fate (vv. 1-4). Luke records, "Peter was therefore kept in prison, but constant prayer was offered to God for him by the church" (v. 5). The church members were fervently praying for Peter during these days. In fact, they gathered in a home and prayed for Peter throughout the night (v. 12).

6. The Antioch Christians prayed for Barnabas and Saul before they left for their first missionary journey (Acts 13:2-3). The proper thing to do before beginning any important effort is to pray for its success and for those involved.

7. On this journey, these men prayed as they strengthened and organized local congregations (Acts 14:21-23). Prayer must play a role in the building up of the local church, as well as in the ordaining of elders and deacons.

Things for Which Christians Should Pray

While the New Testament teaches us to pray for things that are of personal interest to us (daily necessities, forgiveness of sins, guidance, wisdom, etc. – Matt. 6:11-13; James 1:5), this lesson focuses on the things that make praying a good work that helps others.

1. Open doors for spreading the gospel (Col. 4:3). Prayer is an effective tool to use in evangelism. We sometimes lament the fact that no one is interested in hearing the gospel; no one cares. Have we prayed about that? We need to pray for hearts to be open, opportunities to share the gospel with people in our daily lives, and courage to take advantage of these opportunities. We need to make a list of specific people whom we want to see saved and fervently pray for their salvation (Rom. 10:1).

2. Gospel preachers (Col. 4:4). We need to pray for everyone who is involved in the great work of trying to save the lost. Pray for your local preacher. Pray for preachers your congregation is supporting in other places. Pray for the preachers who are holding your gospel meetings, or gospel meetings in your area.

3. The sick—physically and spiritually (James 5:14-16). In verse 16, James promises "the effective, fervent prayer of a righteous man avails much." We are to pray that those who are physically sick will recover, have relief from their pain, receive comfort, etc. We are to pray for those who are spiritually sick, that their hearts would be pricked, they would come to themselves, and repent of their sins.

4. Our enemies (Matt. 5:43-44). This is a very difficult command given by the Lord. The first step in overcoming evil by doing good (Rom. 12:21) is to sincerely pray for those who are causing us harm.

5. Government leaders (1 Tim. 2:1-2). We need to pray that our governing officials will lead with wisdom—that they will lead according to God's will. We are to pray that we can live in peace so that we can busy ourselves with serving the Lord.

Conclusion

Prayer is not like a fire extinguisher – used only in case of emergency. The Christian is to continue earnestly in prayer. There is great power in prayer, but we must put our energy into praying effectively.

We pray for our own interests, but we must also pray for the needs of others. Doing so involves us in a good work, and we are to perform good works with zeal.

Questions:

1. Name two conditions for effective prayer (James 5:16). _____

2. Explain why thanksgiving should be a part of our prayers (Col. 4:2; 1 Thess. 5:18; Php. 4:6; Rom. 1:21). _____

3. What did the apostles do while they waited in Jerusalem (Acts 1:14)? __

4. How did the apostles react to being threatened and commanded not to preach (Acts 4:23-31)?

5. Describe how the Jerusalem church reacted to Peter's arrest (Acts 12:5, 12).

6. Identify some specific ways we can pray for the spread of the gospel. __

7. Why should we pray for our enemies (Matt. 5:43-44; Rom. 12:17-21)? __

8. Why should we pray for governing officials? Consider 1 Timothy 2:1-4 in your answer.

9. What are some things you can do to be more zealous in your prayer life?

Helping the Sick and the Grieving

Lesson 13

We live in a world that suffers from the ongoing consequences of sin. People around us get sick, are injured, undergo surgeries, struggle through rehabilitation procedures, and even lose their loved ones.

Christ intends for us to be zealous for good works. Few works are more needed than going to the aid of those suffering from sickness and/or grief. Unfortunately, some Christians are unprepared to help such people.

Helping the Sick

Jesus expects us to help those who are suffering from illness or injury.

In the Parable of the Good Samaritan, Jesus spoke of a man who had been robbed, beaten, stripped of his clothing, and left half dead (Luke 10:30-37). A priest and a Levite both saw him and continued on their way. In contrast, a Samaritan "went to him and bandaged his wounds, pouring on oil and wine; and he set him on his own animal, brought him to an inn, and took care of him" (v. 34). We are to "go and do likewise" (v. 37).

In Matthew 25:31-46, Jesus painted a picture of final judgment. All of mankind will be divided into two groups. Those on the Lord's right will inherit the kingdom, while those on the left will be cast into hell. Of the saved, Jesus said, "I was naked and you clothed Me; I was sick and you *visited* Me; I was in prison and you came to Me" (v. 36); the lost were told, "I was a stranger and you did not take Me in, naked and you did not clothe Me, sick and in prison and you did not *visit* Me" (v. 43, emphasis mine - HR).

The words *visited* and *visit* are translated from the Greek word *episkeptomai*, which means "to look upon in order to help or to benefit...to look after, have a care for, provide for" (Thayer 242). James used the same word when he said to visit widows and orphans in their distress (James 1:27). This involves more than stopping by and exchanging pleasant greetings. It means checking in on them, determining if they need anything, and doing what we can to help.

Today, there are numerous healthcare professionals (doctors, nurses, ambulance drivers, etc.) who are better qualified than most of us to care for the sick and injured. However, there are still many things we can do to help. We can offer to bring food, take care of household chores, drive them to appointments, or help care for family members.

Helping the Grieving

A loved one's death brings weeping and mourning (Eccl. 3:2, 4). Grief is a gift from God to help us deal with loss; even so, it is one of our most painful experiences.

Local church members should be so close that one person's suffering impacts the entire membership (1 Cor. 12:26). When one or more members lose a loved one, everyone springs into action. There needs to be an immediate outpouring of sympathy. We send cards, flowers, and food. Those who are closest to the family can offer to help with various other things.

God promised to comfort those who are hurting, but this comfort often comes by way of other people who have previously weathered the same, or similar, storms. "Blessed be the God and Father of our Lord Jesus Christ, the Father of mercies and God of all comfort, who comforts us in all our tribulation, that we may be able to comfort those who are in any trouble, with the comfort with which we ourselves are comforted by God" (2 Cor. 1:3-4). Consider the following suggestions when you share comfort with those who are grieving.

1. Be available. It is important to be available for those who are grieving. We can't make the pain go away, but we can be present to help them bear this burden (Gal. 6:2) and support them as they begin and continue the grieving process.

   It is alright to mourn and grieve with them. Jesus did this at the tomb of Lazarus (John 11:35-36).

2. Be understanding. Everyone is different. Just as each person has a unique personality, each also has his own way of mourning the loss of a loved one. Grief does not always unfold in neat, orderly, predictable stages; it can be an emotional rollercoaster. When helping those who have lost loved ones, we may see them at their absolute worst. Most likely, we will witness them expressing extreme, uncomfortable emotions such as anger, despair, fear, and guilt.

   Be ready and willing to "get your hands dirty" as you help during this time. Don't say what they should be feeling. Don't tell them to get over it. Don't challenge or condemn. Let them ride out the storm. Let them know that you are there for them, that they don't have to grieve alone, and that it will get better.

3. Be a good listener. James' instructions, "be swift to hear, slow to speak, slow to wrath," certainly apply in this situation (James 1:19). A listening ear is the best gift you can offer a grieving person.

Job's friends found him and sat with him in silence for seven days (Job 2:11-13). Afterward, Job began to work through his grief verbally. He said some things his friends didn't like hearing. They answered and challenged him, which added to his misery. They didn't become "miserable comforters" until they started talking (Job 16:2).

It can be challenging to sit and listen to a grieving person. People often work through their grief and trauma by talking and telling the same story over and over. This can be tiring for those who are listening, and we may be tempted to try to stop them or get their minds on something else. Allow them to repeat the story. It will help them work through their grief.

4. Think before you speak. "Let your speech always be with grace, seasoned with salt, that you may know how you ought to answer each one" (Col. 4:6). Unfamiliar and uncomfortable situations can cause us to say inappropriate things. We feel the need to say something, grab the first thoughts that come to our minds, and allow them to leave our mouths. Don't do that. If words fitly spoken are like apples of gold in settings of silver (Prov. 25:11), words not fitly spoken can be like arrows shot into the heart (Psa. 64:3-4).

Think before you speak or respond to one who is grieving. Pray about it (Neh. 2:4-5).

5. Maintain support after the funeral. Often, there is an excess of support before and during the funeral, but afterward, everything goes back to normal—except for the one who has lost the loved one. That person is left to find a new normal. As time passes, take the initiative to reach out and check in on them.

Conclusion

Helping the sick, recovering, or grieving is not always a pleasant work, but it is a much-needed work. Let's equip ourselves for this task and make ourselves available to those who need us.

References

Thayer, Joseph H., "Thayer's Greek-English Lexicon of the New Testament," Peabody, Massachusetts, Hendrickson Publishers, 1996, print

Questions

1. Explain why helping the sick and grieving is a good work. _____
   _____

2. What did the Samaritan do for the injured man (Luke 10:34)? _____
   _____
   _____

3. What does the word visit mean, used in Matthew 25:36 and James 1:27?
   _____
   _____

4. What are we to do with the comfort we have received from God (2 Cor. 1:3-4)? _____
   _____

5. When did Job's friends make themselves "miserable comforters"? _____
   _____
   _____

6. What did Nehemiah do when he knew he needed to choose his words carefully (Neh. 2:4)? _____

7. Explain why people grieve in different ways. What factors are involved?
   _____
   _____
   _____

8. Explain why it is important to be a good listener to those who are grieving. _____
   _____
   _____

9. What additional advice do you have to share with those who are helping the sick and the grieving? _____
   _____
   _____

www.ingramcontent.com/pod-product-compliance
Lightning Source LLC
LaVergne TN
LVHW020939090426
835512LV00020B/3431